DEC 2 8 '70

5 ENN 92

P9-CBX-402

12.95

The Poetry of Leaves

A Weatherhill Book • WALKER/WEATHERHILL • *New York & Tokyo*

NORMAN SPARNON

THE POETRY OF LEAVES

Creative Ideas for Japanese Flower Arrangement

MUNICIPAL LIBRARY
MENLO PARK, CALIFORNIA

MP 1

SERIES ANNOUNCEMENT
This is the third volume in Norman Sparnon's series on
Creative Ideas for Japanese Flower Arrangement.
Already published: THE BEAUTY OF WILD FLOWERS
THE MAGIC OF CAMELLIAS (with E. G. Waterhouse)

First edition, 1970

Published by John Weatherhill, Inc., of New York and Tokyo, with editorial offices at 7-6-13 Roppongi, Minato-ku, Tokyo. Distributed in the United States and Canada by Walker and Company, 720 Fifth Avenue, New York, N. Y. 10019; in Australia by Australia & New Zealand Book Company, P. O. Box 200, Artarmon, N.S.W. 2064; and in New Zealand by Whitcombe & Tombs, C. P. O. Box 1465, Christchurch 1. Copyright © 1970 by Norman Sparnon. All rights reserved. Printed in Japan.

LCC No. 70-98336

To
Yuchiku Fujiwara
Grand Master of Rikka

Table of Contents

Introduction

Leaves have always played an important role in the Japanese art of flower arrangement. Their subtle contours, delicate textures, and extreme flexibility give them a unique character of their own. Harbingers of both spring and autumn, with their vivid colors and delicate patterns, leaves are one of the miracles of nature and are considered by the Japanese to be one of the major elements of flower arranging. For centuries the flower masters have produced masterpieces of the art using such leaf materials as aspidistra, lotus, maple, narcissus, and iris. This is to mention but a few of the most favored materials, for there are also many more —the banana leaf, the hosta, the *Rhodea japonica*, and others—that occupy a permanent place of honor in the annals of Japanese flower arranging.

In the present book I have used only sixty varieties of leaves. I did not approach this pleasant task with the object of using as many varieties of leaves as possible: on the contrary, I was strongly tempted to use the same variety of leaves over and over again in many diverse patterns. The great problem, then, was just when to stop. The book could have been devoted entirely to the aspidistra, that beautiful but much maligned relic of the Victorian era. However, for the purpose of variety I have used many others, the majority of which are available in almost all countries.

The few exotic leaves I have used were included for their beautiful variety of patterns and colors and to emphasize the boundless world of this fscinating art. It is not essential to have these exotic leaves in order to do the arrangements any more than it is necessary to have the flax or even the aspidistra. But then I am particularly fond of this latter leaf and believe every flower lover should have at least one of these beautiful plants if only for ornamental reasons.

The purpose of this book is the same as that expressed in the first of this series, *The Beauty of Wildflowers*—to work with whatever material is available and, with the exception of the traditional classical styles, not to imitate. The principles applied in creating the present arrangements can also be applied to any other leaves or flowers. In this book the emphasis is on leaves alone or on arrangements with leaves as their principal material, and in this field the number of beautiful designs that can be created is infinite.

All the arrangements shown are based on the principles of two of Japan's most famous schools of Ikebana—the classical Ikenobo, whose origin dates from the seventh century, and the modern Sogetsu, one of the great schools of this century. Both of these schools place considerable emphasis on the leaf and its adaptability for creative work, and many outstanding examples of the schools' artistry may be seen at their annual exhibitions. Although the basic principles of the two schools may vary, they have certain fundamental precepts in common: to give the arrangement a third dimension, to create asymmetrical balance, to form a design that gives full expression to the material, and to endow the arrangement with feeling.

It cannot be emphasized too much that in order to achieve even a minimum level of competence in flower arranging, a serious study of Ikebana is needed. Sofu Teshigahara, the headmaster of the Sogetsu school, has written: "There are three categories into one of which any artist can be placed. These are: manually competent; outstanding and original; and finally, genius. When one is learning an art, it is an extremely difficult task to attain even the first of these stages." For those interested, a more detailed analysis of the principles followed by these two famous schools may be found in my earlier books.

12   I wish to express a great debt of gratitude to my two teachers—to Yuchiku Fujiwara,

great classical master of the Ikenobo school, who has provided the beautiful arrangement on page 17; and to Sofu Teshigahara, a constant source of inspiration to all serious students of creative Ikebana. I also wish to thank Mr. K. Mair, Director of the Royal Botanic Gardens, Sydney, for his assistance in providing a number of the exotic leaves I have used; Mr. and Mrs. Eric Lowe, of Mosman, Sydney, for giving me access to their beautiful garden; and Mrs. G. Gordon, of Leichardt, Sydney, who provided me with the orchids. Special thanks are due Barbara Forbes, who did all the diagrammatic sketches, and Keith Barlow, Don Cameron, and Miki Takagi who took all of the color photographs.

With the exception of the *rikka* by Yuchiku Fujiwara, all the arrangements are my own. The black-and-white photographs are also my own work.

Leaf Arrangements

1. RIKKA ARRANGEMENT BY YUCHIKU FUJIWARA (Ikenobo). This superb arrangement, by the great classical master and teacher to whom this book is dedicated, is composed of six varieties of leaves arranged in the *rikka* or "standing flower" style, the oldest studied form of Japanese flower arrangement, dating from the mid-fifteenth century. In its original concept, the *rikka* is meant to suggest the ideal of sublimity as represented by the mythical Mount Meru of Hindu and Buddhist cosmology. Known to the Japanese as Shumi-sen, the mountain is symbolized by a skillful combination of several varieties of plant life. A completed arrangement consists of seven distinct features of the sacred mountain: the peak, a waterfall, an adjacent hill, the foot of the mountain, a town, the arrangement's sunlit or *yo* side, and its shaded or *in* side. The last two features are the Japanese equivalents of the Yang and Yin concepts of ancient Chinese philosophy. The harmonious balance of these two—the positive, active, or male principle and the negative, passive, or female principle—is considered one of the fundamental secrets of successful flower arrangement.

In a formal *rikka* these features are expressed in the judicious placement of the following nine principal branches (descriptions of the present arrangement being preceded by dashes): *Shin* ("spiritual truth" or "straight") and *nagashi* ("flowing")—dried sago palm, upper left and lower right. *Soe* ("supporting")—two aspidistra leaves, mid-left. *Uke* ("receiving")—five blades of New Zealand flax, mid-right. *Hikae* ("waiting")—variegated aspidistra leaf, lower left. *Sho-shin* ("sincere," "upright," or "straight")—two variegated aspidistra leaves, center top. *Mikoshi* ("overhanging")—two hanging aspidistra leaves, top right. *Do* ("body" or "trunk") and *mae-oki* ("anterior")—dracaena leaves in body of arrangement.

There can also be various supporting branches: *Kusa-dome* (the last "grass" or flower material to be added)—clipped iris leaves, lower left. *Ki-dome* (the last "tree" material to be added)—three gleichenia leaves, lower right. *Oha* ("large leaves") and *ushiro-gakoi* (branches that finish the arrangement in the rear)—not used here. And *ashirai* (miscellaneous supporting branches), here seen as the *shin-no-uchi-zoe* (a support to the *shin*) and the *soe-no-shita* ("below the *soe*")—single blades of New Zealand flax at the top center and between aspidistra leaves at the lower left.

17

18

THE ASPIDISTRA. In Japanese flower arrangement the *Aspidistra elatior* or, to use its Japanese name, the *haran* (leaf orchid) reigns supreme as "King of Leaves." Its beautiful form, fresh color, versatility, and flexibility make it unsurpassed among all leaf plants, its only possible rival being New Zealand flax. In the Ikenobo, the oldest and most revered of all schools of Ikebana, it is traditional both to commence one's study of the classical styles and also to graduate with the study of this beautiful leaf. Whether it be green, dried, bleached, or preserved (by placing its stem in a mixture of one part glycerine to two parts water), it is infinite in its adaptation.

Some creative ideas for using the aspidistra are: 1) The leaf in its natural form. 2) The leaf trimmed down, achieved by simply trimming the broad side with scissors. 3) Shredding the inner surface of the leaf with the thumbnail. 4) Shredding both sides of the leaf with the thumbnail. 5) Tying the leaf. 6) Furling the leaf and placing the stem over its tip. 7) Furling the leaf and pinning or stapling it. There are also other ways, not shown in the accompanying photograph, such as shredding only one section of a leaf, cutting the top off a leaf, and the like.

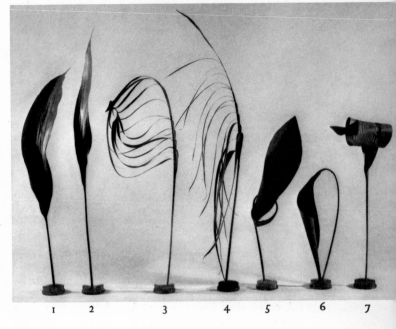

1   2   3   4   5   6   7

◀ 2. FIVE ASPIDISTRA LEAVES (Sogetsu). Five variegated leaves arranged with a rhythmic sweep to give full emphasis to the natural beauty of this remarkable leaf.

19

3. FIVE ASPIDISTRA LEAVES (Ikenobo). Traditionally arranged in groupings of from five to fifteen leaves, an aspidistra arrangement provides a harmony of form and balance inherent in all classical *shoka* styles of the Ikenobo school. *Shoka* is a simplification of the *rikka* style and utilizes only three main branches—*shin* (primary), *soe* (secondary), and *tai* (tertiary), these being the counterparts of the *rikka's shin, soe,* and *nagashi.* Introduced into the Ikenobo school in the eighteenth century, with very few exceptions the *shoka* style uses either one *(isshu-ike),* two *(nishu-ike)* or three *(sanshu-ike)* materials. An analysis of the five-leaf arrangement shown here will provide the serious student with a sound introduction to all subsequent *shoka* styles of this famous school. Let us, then, start at the beginning.

The necessary equipment for this arrangement is: 1) A cylindrical bamboo container known as a *take-tsutsu* or *zundo* is traditionally preferred by the Ikenobo, but any compote type of container is quite in order. 2) A forked twig, known as a *matagi* or *kubari,* for holding the stems firmly in position in the container (see Fig. 2). A needle-point holder may be substituted, but the forked twig wedges the stems more firmly together. 3) A sufficiently large number of leaves to permit careful selection.

Proceed with the following steps: 1) After studying the leaves carefully, divide them into two groups —those that are wider to the left or the right of the central vein (see Fig. 1).

2) From either of the two groups select the straightest and most beautiful leaf. This will be the primary leaf, and its form will determine the style of the arrangement. If, viewing the primary leaf from the back, it is wide left of center, the arrangement will be in the right-hand or *hongatte* style; if wide to the right, then it will be in the left-hand or *higatte* style. (Viewing a completed arrangement from the front, it is easy to determine its style: if the tertiary leaf is at the right, it is a right-hand arrangement, and vice versa.) The arrangement illustrated here is in the right-hand style. The height of the primary leaf may be from one and one-half to three times the height or width of the container.

3) For the *shin-no-ushiro* (the supporting leaf behind the primary), select a leaf from the other group. Its length should be about one-tenth shorter than that of the primary.

4) Select the secondary leaf from the same group as the preceding. When in position this secondary leaf should face the front of the primary. Its length should be about two-thirds that of the primary.

5) For the *shin-no-mae* (the supporting leaf in front of the primary), select a leaf from the same group as the primary. When in position its tip should be below the level of the tip of the secondary.

6) Select the tertiary leaf from the same group as the primary. When in position its front should face the front of the secondary. Because its back is now facing the viewer, its tip is turned slightly down in

order to show part of its front surface. Its height should then be about one-third that of the primary.

7) With the selected leaves, construct the arrangement in the following order: a) the tertiary, b) the supporting leaf in front of the primary, c) the primary, d) the supporting leaf behind the primary, and e) the secondary.

Once the arrangement has been completed, an analysis of its design should reveal the following: 1) The primary stands erect, its back (negative) to the viewer and its tip over its point of origin at the base of the container. Part of the front of the leaf should show at the tip. If, as in the illustration, the wide side is to the left, then the leaf will face to the left, which is known as the *yo* (sun) or positive side.

2) The secondary will appear on the *yo* (sun-positive) side of the arrangement facing the front of the primary.

3) The tertiary will appear on the *in* (shade-negative) side looking to the back of the primary and facing the front of the secondary. An imaginary line drawn from the secondary through the primary to the tertiary should be at an angle of approximately forty-five degrees.

4) The leaf to the back of the primary faces the primary and the viewer; it is on the shade-negative side of the arrangement, in this instance to the right of the primary.

5) The leaf to the front of the primary stands with its back to the viewer facing the primary and on the sun-positive side, in this instance to the left of the primary.

6) It should now be clear that the primary stands as the central axis dividing the arrangement in half from front to rear and from left to right—two leaves to the front and rear, and two to the left and right. The wide, positive side of all leaves is at the left, which is the arrangement's sun-positive side; the narrow, negative sides are at the right or shade-negative side of the arrangement. (See Fig. 3)

Fig. 1. The relative lengths of the five leaves. The white dots indicate the wide side of the back of each leaf. Note that leaves 1, 2, and 3 are wide to the left. Leaf 3 is the primary, 5 the secondary, and 1 the tertiary. Leaves 2 and 4 are the supporting leaves to be placed in front of and behind the primary, respectively.

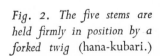

5   4   3   2   1

Fig. 2. The five stems are held firmly in position by a forked twig (hana-kubari.)

Fig. 3. (far right) In the completed arrangement, leaves 1, 2, and 3 show their backs and are wide to the left; 4 and 5 face the viewer and are also wide left of center.

23

4. SEVEN ASPIDISTRA LEAVES (Sogetsu). The elegance of the aspidistra leaf is probably displayed to its full in this design of seven leaves arranged in a manner evocative of the soaring flight of a flock of birds. The asymmetrical pattern is clearly defined in the strong primary line of four leaves supported by the secondary line of two leaves at the left and the tertiary leaf at the lower right.

5. TWENTY-FIVE ASPIDISTRA LEAVES (Ikenobo). In classical Ikebana the Ikenobo school has traditionally limited itself to the arrangement of up to fifteen aspidistra leaves. However, in the freer approach of the modern adaptations of the classical styles no such limitations exist. In this arrangement of twenty-five leaves the basic *rikka* theme has been interpreted with dry rather than the traditional fresh green leaves. The primary rises to the top of the arrangement. The secondary sweeps out to the left, and the tertiary to the lower right. These are the three leaves providing the asymmetrical balance and are the three elements on which all schools and styles of Ikebana are based. In the Sogetsu school these three branches are termed *shin, soe* and *hikae*. The other six primary groups completing this *rikka* are the *uke*, mid-right; the *hikae*, lower left; the *mikoshi*, top right; the *sho-shin*, mid-center; the *do*, the group of leaves in the body of the arrangement; and the *mae-oki*, the leaves protruding to the lower front.

27

28

6. FIFTEEN DRIED ASPIDISTRA LEAVES (Sogetsu). Modern schools of Ikebana observe none of the traditional rules limiting the number of leaves, nor do they give special consideration to the positive and negative aspects of growth. The design is governed entirely by the principles of the school as expressed by the virtuosity of the individual arranger. The Sogetsu places considerable emphasis on form, color, and creativeness. Its great headmaster, Sofu Teshigahara, sees Ikebana as having a close affinity with sculpture. He strongly believes and teaches that we mold floral material in the same manner as a sculptor molds his clay.

The classical principle that an arrangement should seem to rise from its container as a single stem is echoed in this arrangement by the leaves' emerging from one central point, but they rest much lower in the bowl than classical rules would permit. A strong feeling of movement has been achieved by sweeping the leaves in one general direction. Cut at varying lengths for the sake of variety, the subordinate leaves provide asymmetrical balance and support for the three major elements—the primary leaf, rising at the top of the arrangement; the secondary, sweeping down at the mid-left; and the tertiary, lower right. The handsome modern container was chosen for its textural harmony with the leaves.

Dried aspidistra leaves are extremely useful in Ikebana. They may be produced by leaving fresh leaves standing in water for several weeks until they turn brown. They should be removed from the water before the stems decay and then put aside until required. Creases and wrinkles can be easily removed with a hot iron.

7. FIVE ASPIDISTRA LEAVES (Sogetsu). Nature, with all its many aspects, provides myriads of patterns, and one of the joys of Ikebana is the infinite ways it provides for self-expression. The original impetus for any arrangement can come in many ways, now from the container and now from the plant material. In the present arrangement it was the container that provided the idea. The leaves were trimmed to accentuate both form and line. Space was used to underline the idea. The primary leaf soars over the arrangement, following the curve of the container and stabilized by the leaf that crosses it at mid-center. The secondary leaf reaches out on the left, also following the curve of the bowl. The tertiary group sweeps down into and across the bowl, fusing arrangement and container into a single whole.

8. SEVEN ASPIDISTRA LEAVES (Ikenobo). ▶ For an arrangement of seven leaves two leaves are added to the five discussed earlier, one to support the secondary leaf and one to support the tertiary. The length of the leaf to the front of the primary has been raised to a level above that of the secondary. This is a right-hand arrangement.

31

9. TEN SHREDDED ASPIDISTRA LEAVES (Sogetsu). An intricate pattern of interweaving lines has been obtained by trimming one side of the leaf and shredding the other with the thumbnail. The leaves were cut at varying heights and placed in contrasting directions to produce a pattern suggestive of drifting sand. A design such as this could also provide an effective setting for other flowers, but the design is also complete in itself and hence no other material was added in this instance.

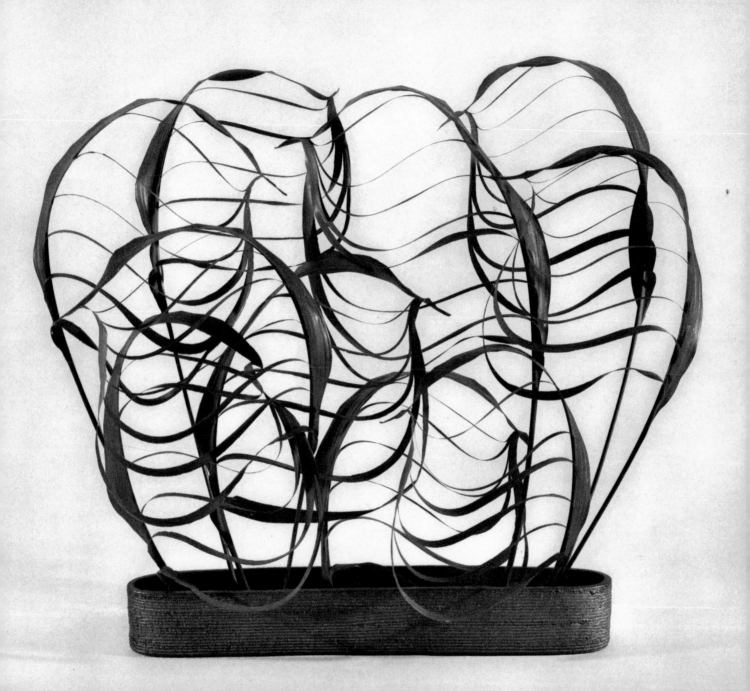

10. FIFTEEN ASPIDISTRA LEAVES (Ikenobo). Poised on the single point of its base, this arrangement might well be named "Arabesque."

In the true classical *shoka* style of the Ikenobo school, the aspidistra is traditionally arranged in groups of from five to fifteen leaves. The present left-hand arrangement consists of the primary group, with seven leaves (the primary plus three supporting leaves to its front and three to its back); the secondary group, with three leaves; and the tertiary, with four. The fifteenth leaf is the short one at the lower left just above the second and third leaves of the tertiary group; it inclines to the lower left rear and is known as the *tai-oku* ("beyond the tertiary").

A completed arrangement of aspidistra leaves should have perfect asymmetrical balance. As explained in the commentary on the five-leaf arrangement, there are always the same number of leaves to the back and to the front of the primary. The primary is the central axis dividing the arrangement from left to right and front to back. A line drawn on the present arrangement from the tip of the primary leaf to the base of the arrangement along its curved axis will show that there are seven leaves to the left of the axis and seven to the right. Similarly, there are seven to the back of the primary and seven to the front. This is the basic formula that requires an odd number of leaves or stems in a classical arrangement.

35

11. FIFTEEN ASPIDISTRA LEAVES (Sogetsu). An entirely different mood has been injected into this arrangement by shifting the weight to the secondary side of the arrangement and molding the leaves into a globular mass form. This globular placement also provides the arrangement with considerable depth. The design consists essentially of two elements, the primary on the right and the secondary on the left. The two are then interwoven by the tertiary grouping at the base. Space is used to emphasize the design, and variety is provided by the contrary movement of the leaves. A shallow plate was used in order to permit full emphasis on the movement of the leaves.

12. FIVE ASPIDISTRA LEAVES (Sogetsu). A ▶ cascading arrangement of five dried variegated leaves in an orange colored container. The arrangement was designed in order to give full effect to these beautiful leaves. The primary group of four leaves cascades down the container, while the single tertiary leaf projects upwards on the right. It is this leaf which gives the arrangement its asymmetrical balance, and also injects variety into the design by contrast of direction.

13. ASPIDISTRA, ROSES, AND HOWEA (Ikenobo). Classical *shoka* arrangements traditionally belonged to one of two categories, according to the number of materials used—*isshu-ike* ("one-material arrangement") or *nishu-ike* ("two-material arrangement"). To meet modern living requirements and allow the arranger more freedom in choice of materials and container, the Ikenobo school has added another category—*sanshu-ike* ("three-material arrangement") —to which the present arrangement belongs. Here the primary and secondary groups are formed with old flower spikes of howea (a type of feather palm). The tertiary group consists of the two full leaves of dried aspidistra and the three roses, the taller leaf being the *do* or "body" of the arrangement. The short clipped aspidistra at the lower left is the *sugata-naoshi* ("body correcting" or "finishing" branch), placed on the positive side of the arrangement under the secondary branch. Although the inclusion of this supplemental branch is not indispensable to this style, it was included here to give stability to the arrangement. Further analysis of the arrangement will reveal that, as in the all-aspidistra arrangements, the tall primary spike provides a central axis dividing the whole in half, the four shorter spikes and the clipped leaf at the rear balancing the roses and leaves at the front.

14. Aspidistra, Wallflowers, and Wisteria Vine (Sogetsu). Leaf plants *(ha-mono)* play a very important role in all schools and styles of Ikebana. The classical styles put considerable emphasis upon the positive and negative aspects of the leaf, whereas modern styles tend to concentrate more upon the front of the leaf. The third basic Sogetsu variation has here been used to express movement. In this variation the primary stem is placed on the left or right of the arrangement with the secondary group on the opposite side. The tertiary group extends directly forward at the base of the arrangement. Variety has been added by the inclusion of wallflowers and peeled wisteria vine. The boat-shaped container is of green glass and provides an interesting balance with the spreading leaves.

15. FIVE BLEACHED ASPIDISTRA LEAVES (Sogetsu). Here five leaves are harmoniously combined in a yellow container. The three tall leaves are arranged to suggest the true meaning of the Japanese term for the primary group, *shin,* meaning "truth, sincerity, uprightness." They stand perfectly erect and endow the arrangement with great dignity. The two supporting leaves are shredded; they both enhance the design and provide a soft contrast for the otherwise austere pattern.

16. FIFTEEN ASPIDISTRA LEAVES (Sogetsu). "Embryo" seems an apt title for these leaves molded together in a manner suggestive of unborn life. This is one of the popular styles of most schools of modern Ikebana, one that places emphasis on mass rather than line. Movement is injected into the design by the intertwining of the leaves in contrary directions. The spaces at the top provide a counterpoint of variety to the heavy mass below and are also suggestive of emerging life.

17. ASPIDISTRA AND SLIPPER ORCHIDS (Sogetsu). In Ikebana an arrangement in a low or flat container is called a *moribana,* as contrasted with one in an upright vase, called a *nageire.* The latter term is derived from the verb *nageireru,* meaning "to throw" or "fling into," and thus suggests the spontaneous casualness of the style, which makes it one of the most popular and beautiful of all styles.

The present arrangement, in a tall terra cotta vase, uses each of three aspidistra leaves in a different way. The primary leaf has been shredded with the thumbnail and cascades down the vase. The secondary is in its natural form and projects to the left with a strong forward movement. The tertiary is furled, its stem inserted through the upper part of the leaf. Two green slipper orchids provide accent.

45

18. NINE ASPIDISTRA LEAVES (Sogetsu). In this design the leaves have been generally arranged in profile in order to vary their pattern. Two contrary movements of direction provide a center of interest at the middle of the arrangement, while the stems on the right provide a harmony of contrast with the leaves on their left. The cut leaf on the left gives variety by way of contrast of shape and provides balance for the tall primary leaf and its supports.

19. FIVE ASPIDISTRA LEAVES (Sogetsu). This pattern of crossed leaves and stems was inspired by the trough-like container. Constructed with a series of repetitive triangular patterns, the design is formal or symmetrical, a style which although quite acceptable is not commonly seen in Ikebana. The design was achieved by holding the tip of the leaf and then twisting the stem. The stem was then placed over the tip of the leaf into the needlepoint holder.

20. THIRTEEN ASPIDISTRA LEAVES (Sogetsu). Here a soaring pattern of leaves has been achieved by cutting the leaves at varying lengths, this time from the base of the leaf. The resulting design is an indication of the infinite variety of patterns to be achieved by mastering the basic principles of a school—a point too often overlooked by students who are apt to follow set patterns or imitate rather than express themselves freely. The arrangement here illustrated is a creative interpretation of the slanting style of the fourth variation of the Sogetsu school. In this style only primary and tertiary branches are used. Here the primary group is composed of the long leaves trailing out to the left front. The tertiary group is the short leaves inclining to the right front.

21. ASPIDISTRA AND BEGONIA (Sogetsu). Five leaves, clipped to dramatize their form, provide an interesting composition of contrasting shapes and sizes. They have been arranged in an asymmetrical three-dimensional pattern by placing them in contrary directions. The tall primary leaf is supported by the leaf that emerges from the secondary group of three leaves at the left. The tertiary group is made up of the two cathedral-window begonias at the base. These two latter elements are not indispensable to the arrangement, but if they had been omitted it would have been better to use a perfectly plain troughlike container. Here the decorated container is in harmony with the colorful leaves.

51

22. ELEVEN BLEACHED ASPIDISTRA LEAVES (Sogetsu). Line is an expressive medium of movement. The rigidity and harshness of straight lines can be made to contrast dramatically with the passiveness and fluidity of undulating curves. The Japanese, masters of line, have for centuries used this medium in all facets of their flower arranging.

Here contrasting spatial areas emphasize the flowing lines and planes of the bleached leaves. Informal balance is achieved by giving accent to the billowing mass. The container is orange colored, with cut-out sides.

23. ASPIDISTRA AND CALLA LILIES ▶ (Sogetsu). This mass-and-line arrangement was clearly inspired by the interesting globular container. An illusion of mass is created by line-enclosed space and is in harmony with the container. The stems, like rods of iron, provide a simple but effective line design. The calla lilies—always excellent flowers for modern Ikebana —provide a striking contrast of color and a center of interest.

53

24. SIX ASPIDISTRA LEAVES (Sogetsu). Rhythm is expressed in this horizontal design constructed in a small black container with cut-out sides. The design consists of two distinct groups of leaves arranged with two contrary movements linked by the tertiary leaf at the base. Design in modern Ikebana requires both imagination and craftsmanship. It was necessary to wire four of the leaves used here in order to obtain stability. The wire was first covered with green floral tape and then carefully attached to the underside of the stem and the midrib of the leaf. In using such artificial aids care should be taken that they are invisible in the completed arrangement.

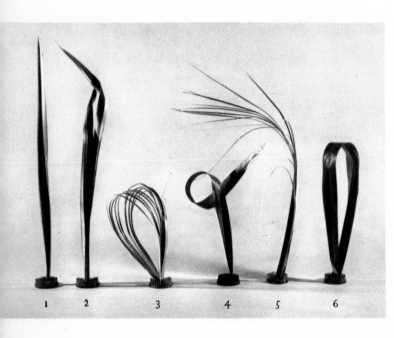

1   2   3   4   5   6

THE NEW ZEALAND FLAX. New Zealand flax strongly rivals the aspidistra in both flexibility and versatility. Because of its beautiful leaf it is highly desirable for all creative Ikebana work, being used either alone or in combination with other leaves or flowers. Native to New Zealand, it is now cultivated in many countries, particulary in Japan, where no classical or modern Ikebana exhibition is complete without a number of flax arrangements. Of the two varieties, *Phormium tenax* is an evergreen that grows from five to seven feet high and has a long, deep green, straplike leaf; *Phormium tenax variegatum* has a beautiful leaf, striped creamy-yellow and white, and is the more popular variety.

Like the aspidistra, New Zealand flax can be twisted, bent, tied, furled, or shredded with remarkable effect. Following are a few creative ideas for using this leaf (keyed to the accompanying photograph): 1) In its natural form. 2) Split down the center and then turned inside out. 3) Shredded with the thumbnail and then looped. 4) The tip threaded through short splits in the leaf. 5) The leaf shredded with the thumbnail or a razor blade. 6) Made into a simple loop.

25. SIX BLADES OF NEW ZEALAND FLAX (Sogetsu). The tall brown vase measuring approximately thirty inches in height provided the motif for the design in this *nageire* arrangement. This design, while similar in principle to arrangements number 27 and 35, evokes a different feeling due to the lack of spatial areas and the concentrated thrust of the blades.

26. NEW ZEALAND FLAX AND CAPSICUM (Sogetsu). This arrangement uses a classical *rikka* theme called *narabi-shin* or "double *shin*," which calls for two *shin* branches of equal length. One of the many *rikka* styles, this is now popular in many schools of Ikebana. The motif is expressed here by the two upright blades of flax supported by variegated capsicum, which provides accent and color contrast. The secondary group of furled flax leaves was made from three leaves split down the center, thus providing narrow ribbon-like blades more flexible for bending. The green container is about twenty inches long.

27. FIVE BLADES OF NEW ZEALAND FLAX (Sogetsu). An orange, cone-shaped container provided the idea for this design. The downward thrust of the swordlike blades is in harmony with the container. The loops enhance the three-dimentional effect and provide variety by way of contrast of direction.

28. NEW ZEALAND FLAX AND DUTCH IRISES (Sogetsu).
A simple slanting-style arrangement of looped leaves
and two yellow Dutch irises for color accent. The
contrary movement of the loops adds a special
interest to the design. The container is of a dull
green color.

29. NEW ZEALAND FLAX AND ANTHURIUM (Sogetsu). ▶
A *shin* or upright style of arrangement with two
blades of flax and an anthurium providing a strong
center of interest. The strong vertical line contrasts
with the loop, which repeats the design of the black
and white container.

63

30. New Zealand Flax and Frangipani (Sogetsu).
Three vases, each about eight inches high, have been asymmetrically grouped to display a handsome frangipani leaf, frangipani flowers, and two flax blades. The long primary blade reaches out to embrace the tall secondary frangipani leaf, which provides a strong contrast of direction. The tertiary group of frangipani flowers provides further variety by way of contrast of color and shape.

31. NEW ZEALAND FLAX, ASPIDISTRA, AND SAGO PALM (Ikenobo). As previously explained, *rikka* is a complex pattern of interrelated parts which, when artfully combined, can produce a work of unsurpassed beauty. The creation of a classical *rikka,* which usually has from seven to nine branches, requires much time, skill, and experience. Because of this and the exigencies of modern living, the Ikenobo school has developed simplified versions of the classical styles. In the simplified *rikka,* for example, there is much more freedom in the choice of materials and the interpretations of designs based on the classical pattern.

The present arrangement is a small modern *rikka* that utilizes a minimum of material and branches. The strong angular blade of flax that rises above the arrangement incorporates the feeling of the classical *shin, soe,* and *mikoshi* branches described on page 16. The two horizontal blades of flax are the *nagashi,* to the right, and the *hikae,* to the left. The sago palm at the right is the *uke,* while the smaller palm branch at the left serves as a support for the *shin-soe* line. The mass of aspidistra leaves at the center incorporates the *sho-shin, do,* and *mae-oki.* These leaves are the ones that were left over after making the arrangement on page 48.

32. NEW ZEALAND FLAX, FAN PALM, AND STOCK (Sogetsu). This is a pattern similar in principle to that of arrangement 38 but with the tertiary area strengthened by the two pieces of clipped palm. The white stock provides a harmonious contrast to the dark green palm leaves. The container is black with cut-out sides.

33. NEW ZEALAND FLAX AND VALLOTA (Sogetsu). Two flax blades soar like elegant birds above a cluster of red vallotas veiled by a shredded blade. To turn a blade inside out, first split it down the center for about three inches approximately nine inches from the top. Holding the leaf at the top of the split to prevent further splitting, thread the tip through the split and pull it erect. The shredding of the leaf is simply achieved with the thumbnail. The modern container is of blue ceramic.

69

34. NEW ZEALAND FLAX AND MARIGOLDS (Sogetsu). Here two flax blades and marigolds are harmoniously combined in a horizontal pattern in a two-hole container. This design also uses the principle of the fourth variation of the Sogetsu school, in which the usual secondary stem is omitted. The principle of the double-*shin* has also been used.

35. ELEVEN BLADES OF NEW ZEALAND FLAX (So-getsu). Entitled "Flight," this arrangement expresses movement by means of the horizontal thrust of the long blades. Although similar in concept to the basic idea of arrangement number 27, here a completely different feeling has been achieved by melding the loops closer together and placing more emphasis upon the blades. These blades are excellent examples of the green, non-striped *Phormium tenax*. The larger leaves were originally about six feet long and four inches wide. They were split down the center and the midrib was removed, thus becoming completely flexible. Each blade was then split with the thumbnail for about one inch and the point of its blade threaded through. Pebbles have been used to conceal the needle-point holder.

36. FOUR SHREDDED LEAVES OF NEW ZEALAND FLAX (Sogetsu). To produce this globular, three-dimensional pattern evocative of steel bands, each of four broad green leaves of New Zealand flax was first split vertically into two halves; then the center ribs were removed to give greater flexibility to the leaves. Each of the eight long half-blades were then cut at various lengths to give variety and then shredded with a number of parallel cuts running from about four inches from the base to within about four inches from the top. Then, one by one, the blades were molded into the desired shapes and fixed firmly on the needle-point holder by folding one end of a blade over its other end.

37. FIVE BLADES OF NEW ZEALAND FLAX (Sogetsu). The flexibility of the flax makes it possible to express many moods. Here a feeling of restfulness is evoked by the free-flowing sweep of the two upright leaves accentuated by the oblique movement of the group of three leaves. The container is an orange trough approximately twenty inches long.

38. NEW ZEALAND FLAX, ORCHID LEAF, AND CALLA LILY (Sogetsu). Simplicity, the substance of many Ikebana styles, is expressed here by a single blade of flax supported by one orchid leaf and one lily in a deep-burgundy-colored glass bowl. With only these three elements it has been possible to express asymmetry, depth, variety of line, and a feeling of mass with the strong flower and the enclosed space.

39. SIX BLADES OF NEW ZEALAND FLAX (Sogetsu). Circles and oblique lines provide the keynote of this arrangement. The circles add variety by way of contrast of shape, give depth to the design, and aid in the transition from the upward to the downward thrust. The container is of a dull green color.

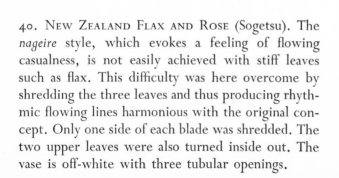

40. NEW ZEALAND FLAX AND ROSE (Sogetsu). The *nageire* style, which evokes a feeling of flowing casualness, is not easily achieved with stiff leaves such as flax. This difficulty was here overcome by shredding the three leaves and thus producing rhythmic flowing lines harmonious with the original concept. Only one side of each blade was shredded. The two upper leaves were also turned inside out. The vase is off-white with three tubular openings.

41. New Zealand Flax and Rose (Sogetsu). Still another mood is here expressed with a minimum of material arranged in the *nageire* style. The two beautiful blades blend harmoniously with the red rose and the modern binocular-shaped container. One leaf has been looped and the other bent over to fall casually down the front of the vase.

42. New Zealand Flax and Everlasting Daisies (Sogetsu). ▶ These four leaves have been treated in the same manner as those on page 80. But the earlier arrangement, using a tall vase, was in the *nageire* style, whereas this, with its low green glass bowl and needle-point holder, is in the *moribana* style. Hence the one has a more erect and vigorous feeling, and the other is more flowing and graceful.

43. SIX BLADES OF NEW ZEALAND FLAX (Sogetsu). A sculptural effect has been achieved by the bold thrust of the blades and the absence of a container, the needle-point holder being concealed by pebbles. The handsome blades are displayed to their full effect with the point of crossing providing a strong center of interest that is off-center to give asymmetrical balance.

44. NEW ZEALAND FLAX, MONSTERA, IVY, AND ANTHURIUM (Sogetsu). A basic upright theme is here employed to display the beautiful form of three different kinds of leaves. The blade of flax stands erect, supported by the monstera leaf, which has been cut in half and provides bold harmonious contrast to the flax. The two leaves are segregated in order to emphasize their forms. The grouping of five leaves of variegated ivy *(Hedera canariensus variegata)* at the base adds variety by way of color contrast and also harmonizes with the round drum-shaped container. The single anthurium flower adds further variety and accentuates the asymmetrical balance of the arrangement.

The trimming or manipulation of leaves to create new designs is a common practice of modern Ikebana. This is the "utilization of nature," as opposed to the purely naturalistic styles in which material is arranged to emphasize its natural growth. Many leaves such as the aspidistra, flax, and monstera become naturally mutilated by the wind while they are growing. By judicious trimming such leaves can assume new forms that inspire stimulating designs. A branch, leaf, or flower is truly in its natural state only while growing. The moment it is cut from its parent body it assumes a new dimension; then, in Ikebana or any other type of floral art, it is the manner in which it is used that defines its artistic merit.

88

45. AN EIGHT-MATERIAL RIKKA WITH NEW ZEALAND FLAX (Ikenobo). Tadao Yamamoto, who died while this book was in preparation, was for many years the chairman of the board of directors of the Ikenobo Institute. He once wrote: "A distinct and common tendency of Japanese culture in general, compared with Western culture, is that the Japanese create beauty through sensuousness while Westerners create through logic. Therefore, logical study of Japanese art, even in the educational sense, is a far cry from the mastery of it. As a matter of fact, even the Japanese, at present, find it easier to understand Western esthetics rather than their own native theories of art because these are so intricate and varied. This is because Japanese art is to be mastered simultaneously through study, practice, and experience. It is not to be understood logically; it is an art to be felt inwardly." I feel quite sure that most Western students of Ikebana will agree with this. But I should like to add that, through study, practice, and considerable experience, one can master the basic principles of *rikka,* which is in fact the essence of Ikebana.

In the present arrangement eight different varieties of material have been used to create a *rikka* that follows one of the traditional patterns. Freedom of expression was found in the choice of the materials and the container. To analyze the parts: 1) *Shin,* two tall blades of flax. 2) *Soe,* monstera leaf, at the left. 3) *Uke,* strelitzia leaf, at the right. 4) *Nagashi,* long branch of *Iresine herbstii,* trailing out to the lower right. 5) *Hikae,* elkhorn leaf, lower left. 6) *Do* and *mae-oki,* gold-dust leaves *(Aucuba japonica variegata)* in the body of the arrangement. 7) *Sho-shin,* short embryo palm, above the gold-dust leaves. 8) *Mikoshi,* tall stem of fern, inclining to the top rear of the arrangement. The fern at the lower right gives support to the *uke.* Note how the whole arrangement rises as a single unit for three or four inches above the top of the container before fanning out. This base, known as the *mizu-giwa* (water's edge), is the critical area of the arrangement.

46. EUCOMIS AND ARALIA (Sogetsu). The versatility of the two-level container is again illustrated in this arrangement of four eucomis leaves and a single leaf of aralia *(Fatsia japonica)*. The primary line is formed by the eucomis at the top level. The secondary and tertiary lines are the eucomis and aralia at the lower level.

47. OLEANDER STEMS AND LEAVES (Sogetsu). This is a spontaneous, simple design dictated entirely by the choice of material—variegated oleander. The rhythmic flowing lines are made possible by the flexibility of the stems, which sweep above a cluster of the colorful leaves. The container was chosen for its harmonious color and because its interesting design is compatible with the space enclosed by the plant material.

94

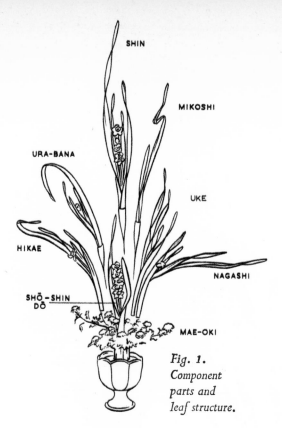

SHIN

MIKOSHI

URA-BANA

UKE

HIKAE

NAGASHI

SHŌ-SHIN
DŌ

MAE-OKI

Fig. 1.
Component
parts and
leaf structure.

Fig. 2. Side view showing depth of arrangement.

THE NARCISSUS. The Japanese rightly consider the narcissus a noble, dignified, and elegant flower, and it has the further advantage of blooming during the cold winter season when other flowers are scarce. The fluidity of line of its beautiful leaves makes it an excellent material for many styles of arrangements, both classical and modern. In formal *rikka* study it is one of the seven materials the student is required to master, each in separate arrangements, the others being pine, cherry blossom, lotus (see arrangement 76), Japanese iris (arrangement 80), chrysanthemum, and maple. As noted in pages that follow, it also plays an important role in the classical *shoka* style.

48. SEVEN-GROUP NARCISSUS RIKKA (Ikenobo). This *rikka* arrangement, approximately three feet high, uses only seven groups of material and hence is smaller than the following arrangement of thirteen groups. It is termed a *suisen nana isshiki,* meaning seven branches of one variety, namely, the narcissus *(suisen).* Despite the "one variety" designation, both the narcissus and the iris *rikka* use a second, accent material for the *mae-oki* at the base, such as the winter chrysanthemums seen here (or another small flower that would have been suitable is the cyclamen), and sometimes also a third material, as in the following arrangement. All *rikka* are roughly globular in form, having both great width and depth

95

(see Fig. 2). As the form of this arrangement depends entirely on the placement of the leaves, they must be carefully manipulated by removing their sheaths and rearranging the leaves to produce the required patterns shown in Fig. 1. The base of the leaves is not visible in the finished arrangement; hence, instead of replacing the sheaths, it is only necessary to rebind the leaves together with green floral tape. Note that in this form the *soe* branch is replaced by a group termed *ura-bana* ("rear flowers") because both leaves and blossoms face directly to the left rear, showing their backs to the viewer. This form also violates another general *rikka* rule in that, unlike the following arrangement, its *hikae* is longer than the substitute *soe*. The small Western-style compote container with grape-vine design is in harmony with this classical arrangement.

49. THIRTEEN-GROUP NARCISSUS RIKKA (Ikenobo). Due to its large number of components, this arrangement is necessarily tall, measuring about five feet high. To obtain this height, the *shin, soe, and uke* groups, in the upper part of the arrangement, have been placed in funnel-like metal tubes that hold them aloft. The *shin* stands high and erect in the center, flanked by the *soe* at the mid-left and the *uke* at the right. The *nagashi* trails out to the lower right, with the *hikae* opposite it. The *sho-shin* and *do* flow down the body of the arrangement, with the *mikoshi* just right of the tall *shin* leaf. Small yellow winter chrysanthemums form the *mae-oki*. The third material used here is the iris japonica, some clipped leaves of which are at the left under the *soe* and at the back of the *shin*. The classical bronze container is in the traditional Ikenobo form called *shi-un* ("purple cloud").

97

50. NARCISSUS AND PHILODENDRON (Sogetsu). Here a basic upright theme is used to reveal the nobility of this lovely flower, which is complemented by a philodendron leaf and arranged in a turquoise container.

99

Fig. 1. *The two groups of leaves.*

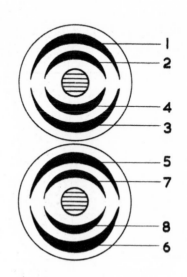

Fig. 2. *Section of the two groups showing method of construction.*

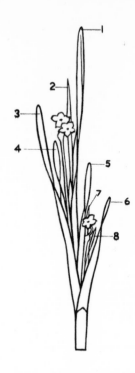

Fig. 3. *The completed arrangement showing the relative positions of the leaves.*

51. NARCISSUS IN A TWO-GROUP SHOKA ARRANGEMENT (Ikenobo). In the classical *shoka* style the narcissus is arranged in two groups, as seen here, or in three, as on page 103. Here one group consists of the primary and secondary branches, and the other of the tertiary. In the primary group, made up of four leaves and one flower, 1 and 2 are the primary, 3 and 4 the secondary. The *tai* group is 5 to 8. The leaves must be rearranged for such arrangements.

Keep the sheath intact by squeezing it softly and removing first the flower and then the leaves. Rearrange the leaves as shown in Fig. 1 and reinsert in the sheath. In the completed arrangement the secondary leaves should incline to the left front, and the sheath holding them together should show just above the lip of the container. This type of arrangement is known as *tomari-bune* or *oki-fune,* depicting a boat in port.

101

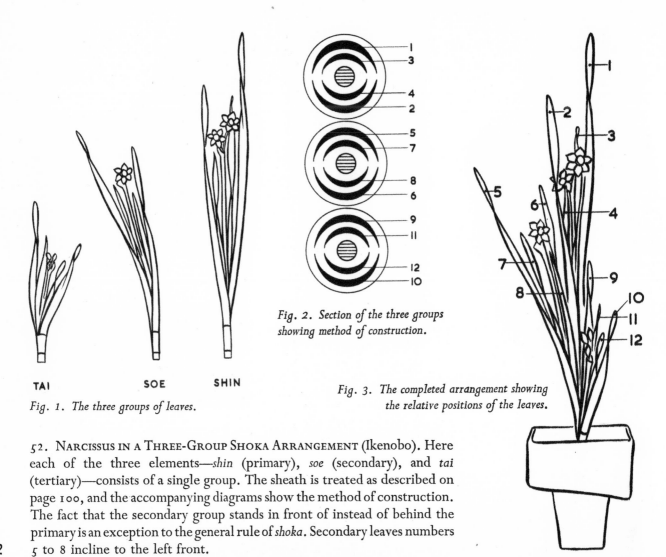

TAI　　　　**SOE**　　　**SHIN**

Fig. 1. The three groups of leaves.

Fig. 2. Section of the three groups showing method of construction.

Fig. 3. The completed arrangement showing the relative positions of the leaves.

52. NARCISSUS IN A THREE-GROUP SHOKA ARRANGEMENT (Ikenobo). Here each of the three elements—*shin* (primary), *soe* (secondary), and *tai* (tertiary)—consists of a single group. The sheath is treated as described on page 100, and the accompanying diagrams show the method of construction. The fact that the secondary group stands in front of instead of behind the primary is an exception to the general rule of *shoka*. Secondary leaves numbers 5 to 8 incline to the left front.

103

53. NARCISSUS (Sogetsu). Here six leaves expressing rhythm and motion embrace a cluster of their flowers. The leaves were shaped by running the blades through the thumb and forefinger.

54. NARCISSUS (Sogetsu). This simple *nageire* arrangement emphasizes the fluidity of the leaves of this lovely flower. The container is a gourd. ▶

55. CALATHEA, ORCHID LEAVES, AND CYMBIDIUMS (Ikenobo). This modern *shoka* arrangement is based on the classical *niju-ike-no-hanagata* or two-level arrangement. At the top, three orchid leaves comprise the primary group; a curved leaf of *Calathea varians,* the secondary; and three cymbidiums the tertiary. On the lower level, the primary and secondary are made up of two orchid leaves, and the tertiary of two cymbidiums. The container is an interesting modern black ceramic version based upon the bamboo container traditionally required for this style.

56. ANTHURIUM AND BEGONIA ▶ (Sogetsu). A blue-green container of modern design provides the setting for these superb leaves of *Anthurium crystalinum* and "Iron Cross" begonia. They are arranged in contrasting directions for visual impact.

57. Anthurium, Calathea, Croton, and Cymbidiums (Sogetsu). The purpose of any good design is to obtain variety in unity. With the exceptions of *rikka* arrangements employing many varieties of materials, most satisfying Ikebana styles usually use not over three kinds of materials. But in the modern styles, which permit much greater freedom of personal expression, there is no rule governing the number of materials: unity is the all-important factor by which any arrangement is judged.

Here, then, is a colorful composition using four different materials. The leaf of *Anthurium andraeanum* forms the primary element, which is supported by two leaves of *Calathea insignis*. The arrangement is completed with two leaves of "Madam Mayne" croton and a cluster of "Irish Melody" cymbidiums.

58. CALATHEA AND CROTON (Sogetsu). Two strikingly beautiful
leaves of *Calathea veitchiana* are
each supported by groups of colorful croton leaves. Harmony of form
and color is the keynote of this
arrangement.

Fig. 1. *The primary group.*

Fig. 2. *The secondary leaf added.*

Fig. 3. *The supporting leaf added.*

59. STRELITZIA WITH FIVE LEAVES (Ikenobo). The forceful lines of the handsome flowers and leaves of *Strelitzia reginae* make a wonderful material for this *shoka* arrangement with its subtle balancing of the positive and negative aspects of Oriental philosophy. The primary leaf (Fig. 1), supported by a flower, is approximately two and a half times the width of the container; it is placed in profile in an upright position with its tip over its base. The secondary leaf (Fig. 2) is about two-thirds the height of the primary and inclines to the left rear facing the primary. The supporting leaf to the front of the primary (Fig. 3) faces the primary and is placed on the positive side of the arrangement. The composition is completed with the tertiary group of two leaves embracing a flower on the negative side of the arrangement.

Fig. 1. The tertiary group.

Fig. 2. The primary group added.

60. STRELITZIA WITH SEVEN LEAVES (Ikenobo). In modern *shoka* a certain degree of latitude is permitted in interpreting basic principles, depending upon the ingenuity, training, and experience of the arranger. For instance, the present arrangement of seven leaves and three flowers violates the traditional rule that there must be an odd number of stems. The primary and secondary groups are each made up of two leaves and one flower; the tertiary, of three leaves and one flower.

In the tertiary group (Fig. 1), two leaves face the flower, with one leaf behind the flower facing the viewer; these four elements are placed to the right of the central axis on the negative side of the arrangement. In the primary group (Fig. 2), which is added next, the tall flower is supported and embraced by two leaves, one to the back on the negative side and the other facing the flower on the positive side, Finally, the arrangement is completed by adding the secondary group, the two leaves facing the primary on the positive side.

As already explained, there are numerous variations on this style of arrangement; for example, the secondary flower could be placed to support the primary flower rather than the secondary leaves. The container is a brown compote.

115

61. STRELITZIA (Sogetsu). In a small, round, two-hole stone container, two leaves are placed at an oblique angle and complemented by a flower for accent.

62. STRELITZIA AND PALM (Ikenobo). This small modern *rikka* uses only three leaves and one flower. With only these few elements a feeling of the grandeur expressed in the more massive arrangements can still be achieved. ▶

63. STRELITZIA (Sogetsu). A pleasing design is here achieved through the blending of verticals and diagonals, which gives full emphasis to both leaves and flowers. The double primary of flowers is supported by the asymmetrical pattern of leaves accented by the flower at the base.

64. THREE TULIPS (Sogetsu). The third Sogetsu variation is used here to provide an interesting pattern for three yellow tulips arranged in a yellow glass container. The primary stem inclines to the left front, the secondary to the right front, and the tertiary extends forward at the center front. The leaves infuse movement and provide contrast of color.

65. Tulips and Monstera (Sogetsu), *far left*. The interesting natural design of two handsome leaves of *Monstera obliqua* provides the highlight of this arrangement. Arranged essentially to display these two leaves, the design is enhanced by the contrary directions of the two elements, the leaves left oblique and the red tulips right oblique.

66. Two Tulips (Ikenobo). One of the aims of the *shoka* style is to give full expression to the natural beauty of one variety of material. In this simple arrangement the two yellow tulips are given full scope to express both their natural growth and beauty. However, it is the leaves which endow the arrangement with its completeness. The primary flower stands erect supported by a leaf to its rear and the secondary leaf on its left. The tertiary group consists of the short flower and the two lower leaves. The asymmetrical balance is found in the scalene triangle formed by the primary flower, the tall secondary leaf at the left, and the tertiary leaf at the lower right. These are the same three branches expressed in the *shin, soe* and *nagashi* of the *rikka* style. This is a right-hand arrangement.

67. LADY PALM AND CYMBIDIUMS (Sogetsu). In this happy and handsome combination of the beautiful "Lady Palm" *(Rhapis excelsa flabelliformis)* and two types of cymbidiums, the lovely spray of "Esmeralda" cymbidiums complements the dark green foliage of the palm leaves, which have been grouped at varying heights to create an interesting pattern of lines. A cluster of "Irish Melody" cymbidiums also complements the leaves at the base of the arrangement. The container, of a gray-green color, is of a type that can also be used for hanging arrangements.

123

68. Bleached Materials and Feather Flowers (Ikenobo). This modern arrangement is based upon one of the nineteen classical styles of *rikka,* the *hidari-nagashi* ("left-hand *nagashi*"), so called because, as an exception to the rule, the *nagashi* is on the same side as the *soe.* In this modern interpretation a blond effect has been achieved by using bleached material with two feather flowers. The *shin* and *nagashi* are the two branches of bamboo at the top and lower left. The *soe* is the fern at the mid-left, which is subordinated to the *uke*—the millet at mid-right—because it appears on the same side as the *nagashi.* The *hikae* is the aspidistra leaf at the lower right. The *do* or body is made up of the honesty, backed by another aspidistra leaf. The *sho-shin* and *mae-oki* are the two feather flowers at the top and bottom respectively. The container was especially designed for modern *rikka.*

126

69. YELLOW CALLA LILIES WITH FAN CORAL (Sogetsu). Here three dramatic elements are combined in a striking design: 1) fan coral, sprayed yellow and black, with its exquisite and distinctive patterns, truly a leaf of the sea; 2) five handsome black-centered yellow callas *(Zantedeschia melanoleuca)*; and 3) a modern black metal container.

Fig. 1. *The five gladioli without their leaves.*

70. FIVE GLADIOLI (Ikenobo). A classical arrangement of five gladioli, such as that seen here, may at first seem primarily a display of flowers. But a comparison of the completed arrangement of leaves and flowers, at the left, with the arrangement before the leaves were inserted, at the right, will show what an important role the leaves play in accentuating the design and giving it movement. The primary group consists of three stems of flowers, the main one with supporting stems to its right rear and left front. The secondary stem inclines to the left rear and the tertiary to the right front. The leaf to the top right rear accentuates the back of the primary line, and the leaves on the left and right accentuate the secondary and tertiary lines. In an arrangement of gladiolus it is preferable to display more buds than flowers as this gives more variety and is expressive of the various phases of existence. The flowers are white and the container turquoise.

71. TWO GLADIOLI (Ikenobo). Whether in the modern or classical styles, or in modern adaptations of the classical, infinite possibilities exist to display the loveliness of the gladiolus and its beautiful leaves. In this version of a renowned classical *shoka* arrangement of only two gladioli stems and their leaves, it is the latter that endow the arrangement with its great character. The principal stem stands erect and dignified, supported by one tall leaf at its right rear and two leaves to its front. The secondary is the tall leaf on the left supported by two shorter leaves. The tertiary consists of the short flower and the leaf to the right front. The flowers are pink and the container gray.

72. MONSTERA AND CARNATIONS (Sogetsu). Both modern and classical schools of Ikebana give considerable emphasis to arrangements in which leaves play the dominant role. Here three monstera leaves have been arranged in contrary directions to add interest to the design. The red carnations provide contrast of color with the green of the leaves and the black and white of the container, with whose shape they are in harmony.

131

73. MONSTERA, CATTAILS, AND CALLA LILIES (Ikenobo). This is a modern arrangement of three materials with classical overtones. The primary group is the three tall cattails that dominate the whole, supported by the secondary branch of the white calla at the left. The monstera leaf forms the *do* or body of the arrangement, and the two white callas form the tertiary group. The container is white glass.

133

74. RHAPHIDOPHORA (Sogetsu). The *Rhaphidophora aurea* was formerly known as *Scindapsis aureus* or golden pothos. Here three of its beautiful leaves of varying sizes are arranged in the *nageire* style in a tall amber glass bottle. These leaves, striking in color and shape, grow freely in subtropical areas.

75. CLIPPED BAMBOO AND AMARYLLIS (Sogetsu). Two containers, one orange and black and the other all black, have been combined into a striking composition harmonious with clipped bamboo sprayed black to blend with the containers. The amaryllis injects variety and provides a colorful accent.

76. Lotus in a Rikka Arrangement (Ikenobo). Emblem of Buddhism, the lotus symbolizes many virtues: propriety, dexterity, elegance, purity, sincerity, and nobility. The present *rikka* arrangement, one of the seven types that, in the main, use but one kind of material, also expresses the three phases of existence—the past by the seed pod, the present by the flower and open leaves, and the future by the bud and furled leaves.

The salient features of the arrangement are: *Shin,* the large open leaf at the top of the arrangement supported by a tightly furled leaf. *Soe,* the furled leaf at the mid-right with the seed pod facing to the rear under it. *Uke,* the open leaf at the mid-left supported by a furled leaf. *Nagashi,* the furled leaf trailing out at the lower left. *Hikae,* the open leaf at the lower right. *Sho-shin,* the tall bud. *Do* or body, the partly furled leaf with its back to the viewer and the flower. *Mae-oki,* the large open leaf extending forward horizontally at the base. *Mikoshi,* the tightly furled leaf at the left of the bud. The yellow pond lily at the left under the *nagashi* is termed the *kusa-dome* or last "grass plant" to be added. The *ki-dome* or "tree plant" is the tightly furled leaf at the lower right.

139

77. NEW ZEALAND FLAX AND TWO TYPES OF BEGONIA (Sogetsu). This simple *nageire* arrangement emphasizes the two lovely leaves of *Begonia rex*— "Salamander" to the left and "His Majesty" to the right.

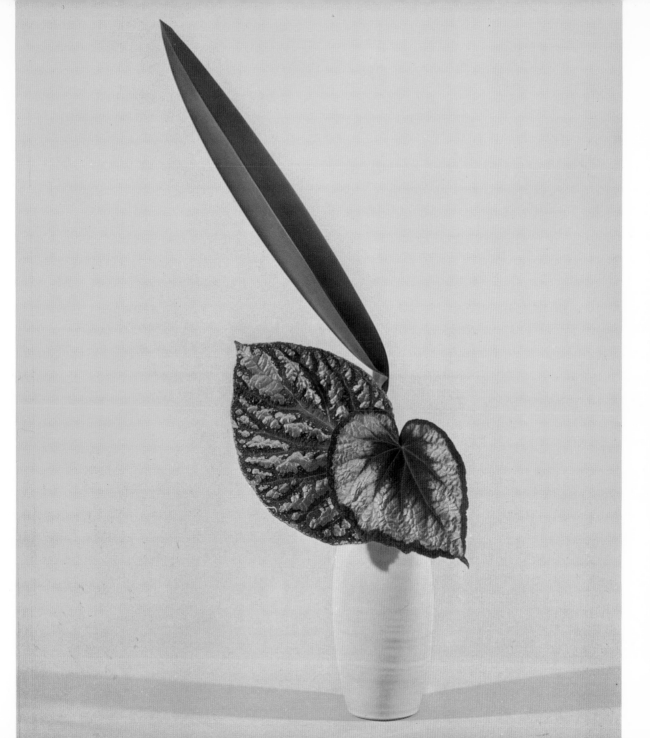

78. ARALIA AND REGAL LILY (So-getsu). The leaves of aralia *(Fatsia japonica)* have been clipped and arranged in an open style to give full emphasis to their form and line. The *Lilium regale* accentuates the asymmetrical pattern and provides a contrasting accent. The modern two-hole container is of a blue-green color.

144

79. IRIS ENSATA (Ikenobo). A cursory study of this extremely beautiful iris by any student of Ikebana will reveal that the success of its arrangement depends on an understanding of the placement of its leaves. The Japanese are not much given to horticulture, at least not as we understand the term in the West. This is due no doubt to the fact that they do not have the home gardens with the profusion of flowers that we do. But when it comes to Ikebana, they most certainly know the habit and essential spirit of plants probably more than most horticulturalists. For confirmation one has only to look at their arrangements of such plants as the aspidistra, *Rhodea japonica,* the day lily, the narcissus, and many others, not the least of which is the iris.

In arranging the iris every care must be taken to ensure that the leaves are grouped to express their natural growth. In the present classical *shoka* arrangement a minimum of leaves and flowers has been used.

The method of construction can be readily understood by referring to the accompanying sketches. Leaves 1 and 2 comprise the tertiary group; 3–5, the primary; and 6 and 7, the secondary. Only in the case of number 1 are the leaves arranged in their natural grouping of three blades; thereafter they are arranged either singly or in groupings of two. Being essentially a summer flower, the flowers rise above the leaves.

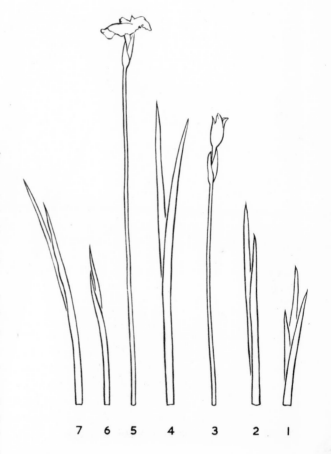

7   6   5   4   3   2   1

145

80. JAPANESE IRIS (Ikenobo). As previously noted, the original purpose of the *rikka* style was to express nature in all its grandeur and majesty. The style is a beautiful study of the subtleties of complete form: it is a perfect balance of interrelated parts that, when harmoniously combined, provide a pattern that is perfectly complete in itself, needing precisely nothing more and nothing less. A full understanding of *rikka* principles can produce a work that, even with various subtle omissions and departures from the rules, is fully faithful to the original concept, one that embodies all the principles necessary for the study of good Ikebana.

The iris is perhaps the most beautiful of the seven materials used in making *rikka* arrangements consisting principally of but a single material, and its successful arranging is surely one of the most rewarding experiences in all of Japanese flower arranging. The present arrangement of the Japanese iris *(Iris laevigata)* clearly defines the salient *rikka* features previously explained. The pond lily at the base of the arrangement is an accessory included for accent.

147

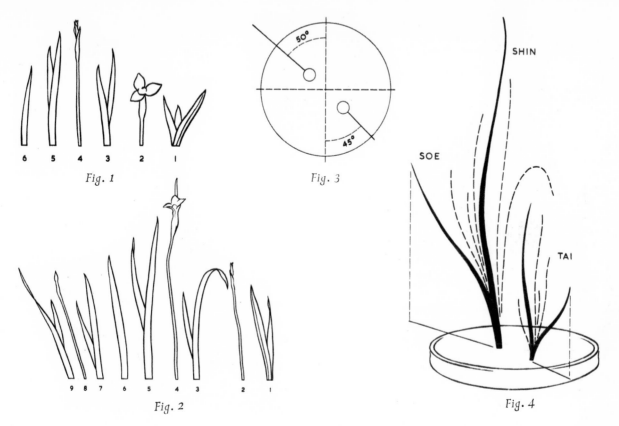

Fig. 1

Fig. 3

Fig. 2

Fig. 4

SHIN

SOE

TAI

81. JAPANESE IRIS (Ikenobo). The *gyodo-ike* or "Fish Path" arrangement illustrated here is one of the renowned styles of classical Ikebana. It is made in two parts and uses either one or two varieties of water plants—great reed and iris, iris and pond lily, bulrush and iris, etc. A somewhat similar style is termed *suiriku-ike* or "Water and Land" arrangement, in which a dividing stone is used in combination with a water and a land plant.

The six leaves of Fig. 1 comprise the tertiary or *tai* group; only number 1 is arranged in a grouping of three. Note that its center blade is shorter than the other two, whereas it is longer in the arrangement on page 144. This is because of the different growth habits of the two types of iris used in the respective arrangements.

In Fig. 2 the number 1 group is known as the *tai za,* meaning the normal position of the *tai*. Numbers 2–6 are the primary or *shin* group, and numbers 7–9 the secondary or *soe* group.

Figs. 3 and 4 show the relative positions of the groups in the bowl.

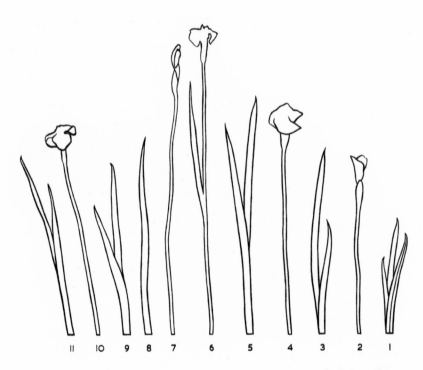

Fig. 1. *Breakdown of the arrangement, the numbers indicating the order of arranging.*

82. IRIS ENSATA (Ikenobo). This *shoka* arrangement uses five flowers and six groups of leaves. Numbers 4–8 are the primary group; 9–11, the secondary; and 1–3, the tertiary. Again only number 1 is arranged with three blades; this is because it is the group that is most clearly visible to the viewer and hence reveals the natural growth of the plant, whereas in the profusion of leaves and flowers in the rest of the arrangement it is not possible to tell how many blades have been used in any one grouping.

151

83. IRIS ENSATA (Sogetsu). The swordlike blades of this type of iris make it the traditional flower for Boys' Day, celebrated on the fifth day of the fifth month.

Unlike the classical styles, in which great care is used in grouping the leaves, in modern Ikebana the principal emphasis is on a spontaneous grouping of both leaves and flowers. But both styles have one point in common: the desire to express the natural beauty of this lovely flower to the fullest extent.

In this double arrangement, buds and flowers rise above free-flowing leaves arranged to evoke their natural growth.

84. PHILODENDRON, ALOCASIA, AND CALLA LILY (Sogetsu). The purpose of this design is to show the beautiful form of the two leaves. The *Philodendron imbe* soars over the *Alocasia cuprea,* and the white calla lily provides a contrasting but harmonious link between the two. The container is a green compote.

153

85. A SEVEN-MATERIAL RIKKA (Ikenobo). The *rikka* style was formalized by the Ikenobo masters in Japan at the time of the Renaissance in Europe, and for some three hundred years it reigned supreme as the "king" of Japanese flower arrangements, being much favored by Buddhist priests, the nobility, and samurai. Although very beautiful, it nevertheless became somewhat stereotyped as rules proliferated governing the smallest details in the placement of branches and the types of materials to be used. In the end its popularity was eclipsed by the simplified three-branch *shoka* style that arose in the eighteenth century and again by the still freer *moribana* style introduced early in this century. At present, however, due to the completely free approach to Ikebana that has swept Japan during the past two decades, the *rikka* is enjoying its own renaissance in modern, freer variations. Freedom of choice in the use of materials and containers and imaginative placement of the branches, although inspired by classical examples, have been responsible for its great and popular revival in recent years.

In the present modern *rikka* seven kinds of materials are used to interpret the nine primary branches which constitute a traditional *rikka*. The *shin* or primary branch is the tall spray of cymbidiums that soars over the arrangement. The *soe, uke,* and *do* are formed with the beautifully natural fish-shaped leaf of the palm *Chamaedorea ernesti augusti*. The *mikoshi* or overhanging branch is the graceful cymbidium leaf. The *sho-shin* is the two yellow Dutch irises at the center. The *nagashi* or flowing branch is the leaf of *Anthurium scherzerianum* at the lower right, balanced by a *hikae* of an aspidistra leaf on the opposite side. The *mae-oki* or anterior branch is the leaf of *Monstera obliqua* at the base of the arrangement. The old classical bronze container is in complete harmony with the modern lines of this arrangement.

155

86. ANTHURIUM, MONSTERA, AND SHELL GINGER (Sogetsu). The two leaves, the anthurium above the monstera, are linked by the two graceful sprays of shell ginger (*Alpinia speciosa*) arranged in a white glass bowl.

87. ALOCASIA AND ANTHURIUM ▶ (Sogetsu). The dramatically beautiful leaf of the *Alocasia amazonica* does not express the spontaneous casualness usually inherent in the *nageire* style used here. But the harmony between leaf and container gives the leaf its full majestic dignity. The interesting anthurium (*Anthurium scherzerianum*), like one of nature's caricatures, provides a contrast of both color and form and complements the drama of the leaf.

157

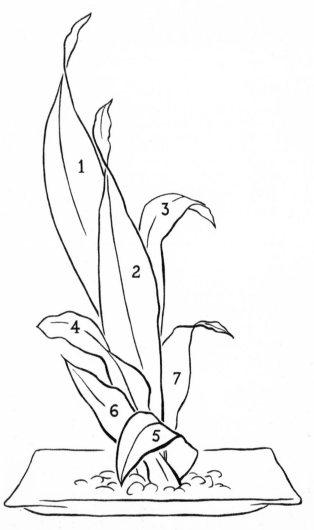

88. DRACAENA (Sogetsu). This closely knit composition of seven dracaena leaves is in the *moribana* style but has a strong classical feeling. The gradation of the leaves adds interest to the design, and a feeling of movement is suggested by inclining the whole arrangement slightly to the left front. The glass container was chosen for its harmony of texture with the leaves. The accompanying sketch shows the method of construction.

159

89. KANGAROO PAW AND VERTICORDIA (Sogetsu). The dark green straplike blades of kangaroo paw contrast vividly with the mass of golden verticordia *(Verticordia nitens)*. As a minimum of elements were to be used, each was carefully chosen for the role it was to play in the completed design—the flower for its contrast of color with the leaves, and the container for its harmony of color with the flower mass and its strong horizontals, which contrast with the oblique lines of the leaves.

161

90. Wisteria Vine and Three Types of Begonia (Sogetsu). The spectacular *Begonia rex* "Pink Curl" is flanked by the begonia "Cleopatra" on the left and the *Begonia rex* "His Majesty" on the right. The wisteria vine provides a little variety without detracting from the leaves.

163

164

Fig. 1. The tertiary group.

Fig. 2. The primary flower and leaf added.

91. CANNA (Ikenobo). One of the most common of flowers, the beautiful leaves of the canna make it particularly well suited for arrangements in the classical *shoka* style. Here the tertiary group (Fig. 1) consists of one stem of flowers and three leaves; the primary flower (Fig. 2) is supported by a leaf to its rear; and the arrangement is completed with the addition of the secondary leaf at the left.

92. CALLA, ASPIDISTRA, MONSTERA, AND NARCISSUS (Sogetsu). Mass and line are here achieved with a harmony of contrasting leaf shapes and graceful natural forms blended together and accented with a cluster of narcissus. The aspidistra leaf has been lightly trimmed to accentuate its form. The container is of a blue-green color.

93. MACROZAMIA PALM (Sogetsu). ▶ The palm stems were clipped, gently curved with the fingers, and then arranged in an intricate pattern of lines expressing movement, the varying spatial patterns and groupings of the ends providing variety. The container is green and white.

167

94. DRIED MONSTERA (Sogetsu). As in this bizarre arrangement of two monstera leaves, many dried leaves provide interesting and stimulating patterns for modern Ikebana. Using only two design elements—in this instance a primary and a tertiary branch—one can achieve an infinite variety of results. The brown-and-black container was chosen for its textural harmony with the leaves.

95. GLEICHENIA AND DAFFODILS (Sogetsu). A pleasant design has been achieved here by arching the five pieces of fern at varying heights and accenting them with a column of three daffodils. The container is orange colored. ▶

169

96. SANSEVIERIA (Sogetsu). Commonly called mother-in-law tongue, the sansevieria blade offers limited flexibility for creative designs but is nevertheless capable of interesting variations. Here two blades have been split and turned inside out. Further variety is introduced by varying the heights and contrasting the direction of one of the blades.

97. SANSEVIERIA (Sogetsu). Here ▶ the blades have been cut at varying lengths and arranged obliquely to create a pleasing pattern. The modern container is very harmonious with the plant material both in design and texture.

171

98. SANSEVIERIA (Sogetsu). "Chorus" might be an apt title for this design. Japanese flower arrangers often give such expressive titles to their finished arrangements, though the opposite procedure of choosing a theme and then creating an arrangement to fit it is seldom followed. As in most contemporary art forms, principal emphasis is on creative work based on the mastery of basic principles rather than on literary conceits.

Here five blades have all been split, turned inside out, and arranged on a horizontal plane. The varying heights provide informal balance.

173

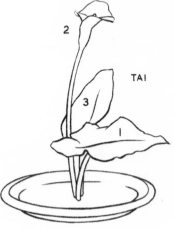

Fig. 1

99. WHITE CALLA LILY WITH
FIVE LEAVES (Ikenobo). Like
other materials used in classical leaf arrangements, the
calla has its own special set of
rules. It is usually arranged in
odd numbers of from five to
nine leaves, the five-leaf form
being probably the most popular. An analysis of the present arrangement of five leaves
and two flowers of the white
calla *(Zantedeschia aethiopica)*
follows:

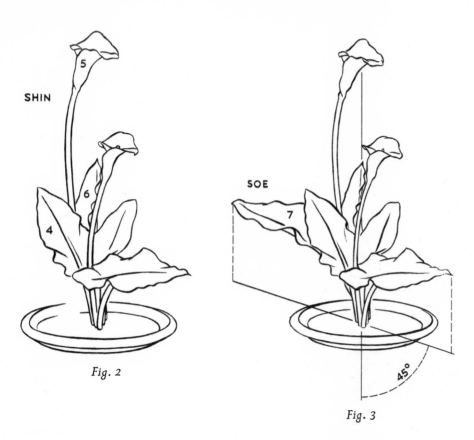

SHIN

5

6

4

Fig. 2

SOE

7

45°

Fig. 3

7　6

5

4　3

2

1

Fig. 4

Fig. 1. The tertiary or tai group consists of two leaves embracing a flower and is placed on the negative side of the arrangement.

Fig. 2. The primary or shin group consists of leaves 4 and 6 embracing the flower 5. Leaf 4 is on the positive side.

Fig. 3. The secondary or soe group is leaf 7. Note how the primary flower stands over its point of origin at the base. A vertical line drawn from this flower to its base touches the edge of the tertiary flower and passes through the tip of the leaf to the back of the primary.

Fig. 4. The positions of the various elements in the needle-point holder.

175

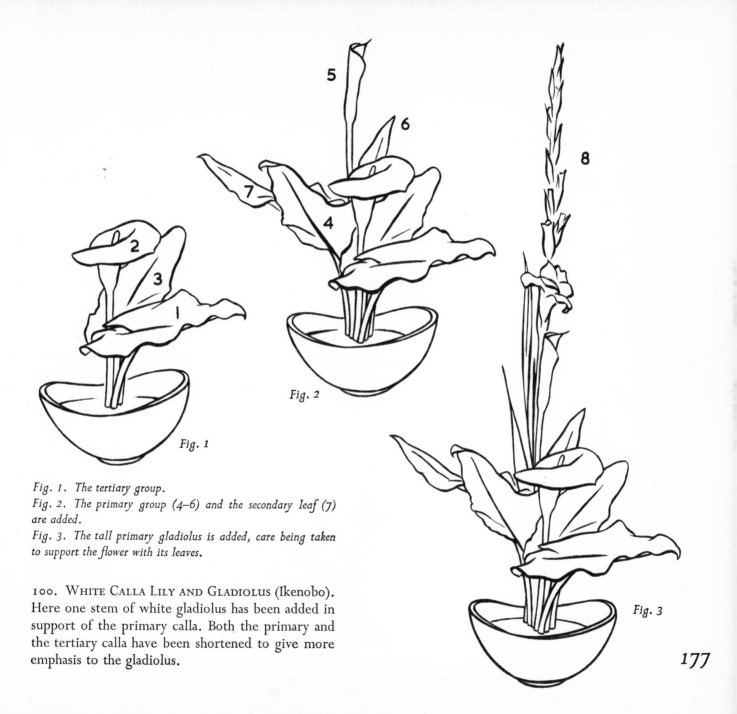

Fig. 1. The tertiary group.

Fig. 2. The primary group (4–6) and the secondary leaf (7) are added.

Fig. 3. The tall primary gladiolus is added, care being taken to support the flower with its leaves.

Fig. 1

Fig. 2

Fig. 3

100. WHITE CALLA LILY AND GLADIOLUS (Ikenobo). Here one stem of white gladiolus has been added in support of the primary calla. Both the primary and the tertiary calla have been shortened to give more emphasis to the gladiolus.

101. WHITE CALLA LILY WITH SEVEN LEAVES (Ikenobo). In an arrangement of seven leaves and two flowers, the primary group consists of two flowers and three leaves; the secondary and tertiary, of two leaves each. The tall primary leaf stands with its back to the viewer supporting the two primary flowers, forming the central axis dividing the arrangement into three leaves on the left or positive side and three on the right or negative. The shorter flower stands to the rear of the taller.

102. CLIPPED PALM (Sogetsu). Infinite patterns can be achieved with clipped palm leaves. Here the strong vertical, the gentle curve, and the two lower discs form a pattern in complete harmony with the black gondola-shaped container. Further variety is provided by the vertical, horizontal, and oblique planes of the leaves.

103. CLIPPED PALM IN A TWO-GROUP ARRANGEMENT (Sogetsu). Two groupings of pleasantly proportioned masses are used in this arrangement to emphasize two of the important ingredients of modern Ikebana—line and mass.

104. CLIPPED PALM IN A RIKKA ▶ ARRANGEMENT (Ikenobo). The "left-hand *nagashi*" of the *rikka* style is here interpreted with a modern feeling by using only palm leaves. In a conventional *rikka* the *nagashi* would be on the negative side and the *soe* on the positive, whereas here both are on the positive side, which is to the left. Hence the two *shin* leaves curve slightly to the left as though drawn by the sun. The *soe,* the short palm leaf at mid-center, normally plays a more dominant role but has here been subordinated to both the *nagashi* and the *uke* for better balance. The *uke,* at the mid-right, has been lengthened to balance the *nagashi* at the lower left. The container is dull orange and gold with a black lining.

181

105. WATSONIA AND CALLA LILY
(Sogetsu). In this line arrangement
the watsonia leaves provide a contrast of direction while the calla
lily provides the center of interest.
The container is blue.

106. BLEACHED PHOENIX (So- ▶
getsu). Four bleached phoenix
leaves were looped and then placed
in contrary directions to produce
this dramatic design emphasizing
the natural lines of the palm. The
container is dull orange and gold
with a black lining.

183

107. TREVESIA AND LILIES (Sogetsu). The wizardry of nature is fully displayed in the natural design of these superb leaves of *Trevesia palmata micholitzii*, which resemble mammoth snow crystals. They have been arranged in a tall brown vase to give full emphasis to their beautiful patterns and highlighted with a cluster of *Lilium longiflorum*, which compliments rather than detracts from the grandeur of the leaves.

The Preservation of Leaves

The methods for preserving cut leaves and flowers are many and varied. They are the results of experimentation by numerous flower lovers throughout the world, and many of them have proved very successful. The few hints offered here have been used over a long period of time, both in Japan and in other countries, with considerable success. For other methods and more detailed information see the first appendix in my earlier book, *Japanese Flower Arrangement, Classical and Modern*.

The more popular methods may be divided generally into the following four categories:

1) CUTTING IN WATER (*mizu-giri*). This is the most popular and time-proven Japanese method for prolonging freshness for several days. *Mizu-giri* means literally "water cutting," which is to say the cutting of stems while they are immersed in water. This is an extremely effective way of keeping the stems from absorbing air and of stimulating suction. The stem should be immersed in a bowl of water and approximately one-half inch cut off while under the water. After cutting, hold the stem in the water for another few seconds and then either transfer the leaf or branch to another water-filled container, where it may be left standing for a few hours, or else proceed immediately to arrange it in a flower container that already has water in it. If the leaves have been freshly cut from the garden, it is preferable that they be left standing in fairly deep water for several hours before being arranged, and they should be cut under water once more when doing the arrangement. Leaves such as those of the castor-oil plant, caladium, and begonia react very quickly to this treatment.

2) IMMERSING IN GLYCERINE. This is another popular and effective method for preserving leaves over a longer period of time. Prepare a mixture of two parts water and one part glycerine, thoroughly mixing the two liquids together in a jar. After carefully cleaning the surfaces of the leaves, make several vertical cuts in the ends of the stems and put them in the mixture to a depth of about five inches. The period of absorption varies according to the nature of the plant and may take from two to five weeks or, in the case of leaves like the aspidistra and dracaena, much longer. Different tones of coloring can be achieved by controlling the period of immersion. Experimentation is the best method for determining which leaves will be best preserved by this method,

but it has been found quite effective in the following cases:

aralia	eucalyptus	magnolia
aspidistra	fatshedera	mahonia
beech	ficus	oak
birch	ivy	oleander
camellia	juniper	pittosporum
crab apple	laurel	privet
dracaena	loquat	rhododendron
elaeagnus		

3) DRYING. The method I have found most effective for drying leaves is to leave them standing in water for rather lengthy periods. In this way they dry gradually. Aspidistra leaves start turning brown after several weeks and later turn a beautiful golden brown. They can then be stored until needed in a box or rolled up in paper. Should they become creased, they can be made smooth again with a hot iron, but care should be taken not to crush the center vein. Monstera and strelitzia leaves will take on interesting forms if left to dry gradually in water. When drying leaves, it is best not to leave too much water in the container; in this way the leaves will gradually absorb all the water as they dry out. But if much water is needed, care should be taken to see that the stems do not decay. Some other leaves that dry effectively are those of the banana, sago palm, and tetrapanax papyriferum.

4) BLEACHING. Japanese florists have been bleaching many types of plants, ranging from millet to sunflowers, with outstanding success for many years, and their products are now being widely exported. Hence much bleached material can be easily bought, thus obviating the necessity of doing one's own bleaching, a process that entails using acids or sodas that can be harmful to the skin, to children, and to pets. However, limited success can be achieved by using any of the commercial bleaches in boiling water. The plant material must remain immersed until all the color has come out. It is then washed under cold water and hung out in the sun for further bleaching and drying. Popular bleached-leaf plants in Japan include the bamboo, aspidistra, palm, sago palm, and fern (*Gleichenia linearis*).

Index

The "weathermark" identifies this book as having been planned, designed, and produced at the Tokyo offices of John Weatherhill, Inc. Typography and book design by Meredith Weatherby. Layout by Naoto Kondo. Composition by General Printing Co., Yokohama. Plates, in five-color offset and monochrome gravure, engraved and printed together with the text by Nissha Printing Co., Kyoto. Bound at the Okamoto Binderies, Tokyo. The type face used is Monotype Perpetua, with the introductory text in fourteen point and the captions in twelve.